MW01711574

COMPULSIVE CONSUMPTION

6 STUDIES FOR WOMEN ON MATERIALISM

DR. JUDY HAMLIN

VICTOR BOOKS
A DIVISION OF SCRIPTURE PRESS PUBLICATIONS INC.
USA CANADA ENGLAND

Scripture quotations are from the Holy Bible, New International Version®. *Copyright © 1973, 1978, 1984 by International Bible Society. Used by permission of Zondervan Publishing House. All rights reserved.*

Copyediting: Jane Vogel
Cover Design: Scott Rattray
Cover Illustration: Robert Bergin
Interior Illustrations: Al Hering

Recommended Dewey Decimal Classification: 243.833
Suggested Subject Heading: BIBLE STUDY: WOMEN
Library of Congress Catalog Card Number: 93-28587
ISBN: 1-56476-196-7

1 2 3 4 5 6 7 8 9 10 Printing/Year 97 96 95 94 93

VICTOR BOOKS
A division of SP Publications, Inc.
Wheaton, Illinois 60187

CONTENTS

To my loving, patient husband, who has now lived for 27 years with the girl in red shoes.

INTRODUCTION

At age 12 I rode a city bus to town, went to a department store, charged two pairs of shoes without a charge card, and returned home.

It is no wonder that, newly married at 19 and strapped for money as are most young couples, I came home and proudly told my husband I had bought the prettiest red shoes and handbag. His reply was, "How did you pay for them?"

My answer: "I didn't have to pay for them. I charged them!"

Naive? Yes. A lot to learn? Of course. Were the lessons easy? No! Did they take time? Heavens, yes.

My prayer is that God's Word and your group's experiences will help you overcome compulsive consumption.

Each session in this study includes:

- ☐ *Scripture* and *Purpose* statements that reflect the goals of the session.
- ☐ *Looking Inside*, combining questions with illustrations to be used as conversation starters.
- ☐ *Topical Text* that prompts participants to work through specific issues.
- ☐ *Scriptures* that speak to those specific issues.
- ☐ *Praying Together*, which encourages participants to develop the discipline of prayer and praise.

In the *Leader's Notes* you will find background information, additional questions, and an outline for each session. During the course of this study the Holy Spirit might prompt you to make a decision to receive Jesus Christ as your Lord and Savior. If this happens, turn to the back of the study and review the Five Steps. You may do this alone, with a friend, or with your group leader. Record your spiritual birthday, then read, claim, and receive God's gifts.

CONTENT

DISAPPOINTED

PROUD

ANXIOUS

AMBIVALENT

HAPPY

RESENTFUL

ENVIOUS

SEARCHING FOR ANSWERS

1

MYSELF—WHO AM I?

SCRIPTURE
"For where your treasure is, there your heart will be also" *Matthew 6:21.*

PURPOSE
To enhance our awareness of how we see ourselves.

LOOKING INSIDE
1. Which emotion(s) illustrated on the opposite page best describe(s) how you usually feel about yourself? Is that self-concept tied to how your needs and wants are being met daily?

2. Which illustrate(s) the way you would like to feel?

3. Have you ever felt that it would be good for you to think less about "things"? Why do you think so?

ARE YOU A SHOPAHOLIC?
"Ten to thirty percent of the population are shopaholics—people who shop compulsively to relieve inner distress," according to Candace Walters ("When Mallmania Strikes," *Today's Christian Woman,* vol. 11, no. 6, November/December, 1989, p. 45).

Are you in that group? Take several minutes to respond to the following questions. Your leader will help you evaluate your response to the list.

- ☑ Are you driven to shop, even when you don't have the time or money?
- ☑ Do you head for the mall when you feel depressed, disappointed, angry, or lonely?
- ☑ When you shop, do you have feelings of elation mixed with uneasiness?
- ☐ Do you find it hard to resist a sale, or do you buy things you don't want or need because the bargain is "too good to pass up"?
- ☐ Are many of your purchases seldom used or never opened?
- ☐ Do you hide items you have bought, or lie to your family and friends about your purchases?
- ☑ If you have excess money, are you obsessed with spending it?
- ☐ Do you divert money from paying bills to use for shopping excursions?
- ☐ When you return home after shopping, do you feel guilty, confused, or try to justify your spending?
- ☐ Do you buy merchandise with credit cards that you would not buy with cash?
- ☐ Are your spending habits emotionally disturbing to you, or causing a conflict between you and someone close to you?
- ☐ Do you get upset if an unexpected chore, call, or emergency interferes with your shopping plans?

(Walters, p. 47)

OVERCOMING

As a group, review the following list of ways to overcome compulsive shopping. Stop to discuss any methods that group members have used.

1. Analyze why and when you shop.
2. Compare your imagined gains with your actual losses.
3. Make a list and set a time limit for your shopping excursions.
4. Use your credit cards wisely or pay in cash.
5. Develop relationships that will fill your need to socialize.
6. Avoid department store sales.
7. Examine your value system.
8. Don't be afraid to get professional help.
9. Reward yourself for your progress.

(Walters, pp. 46, 86)

WHAT DEFINES YOUR IDENTITY?

Circle those things you feel help define you:

THINGS	BODY	PEOPLE & ANIMALS
Clothing	Body weight	Spouse
Car	Hair	Pets
Jewelry	Eyes	Parents
House Furnishings	Signs of aging	Children
Credit cards	Nails	Employer
Heirlooms	Legs	Siblings
	Physical fitness	Friends

TAKE FIVE

With your neighbor, take five minutes to discuss what rank the above three categories hold in your life. List them first, second, and third.

1st PEOPLE + ANIMALS

2nd THINGS

3rd BODY

PITFALLS

Take time to list, by category, the pitfalls of assessing ourselves by what we possess. (For example, under "THINGS" you might list "envy," "greediness.")

THINGS	BODY	PEOPLE & ANIMALS

As a group, discuss your lists, adding to them as you go.

MATERIALISM

Steve Thurman, in "Life, Liberty and the Pursuit of Just a Little More" (*Discipleship Journal*, vol. 9, no. 5, September/October 1989, p. 27), defines a materialist as

> someone who is preoccupied with the things of this world, cares too much for the things that can be purchased, spends his days dreaming only of the next acquisition. And he is frustrated if he can't get what he wants when he wants to have it. 'For the materialist, life is a preoccupation with jewelry, or landscaping, or remodeling the home, or trips abroad, or nice cars, or a business deal. Life revolves around these things. He is obsessed with the "stuff" of life. And in the midst of it all, where is Jesus? He is quietly and politely set aside. Like Martha in Luke 10:38-42, the materialist is "distracted" from his Lord and "worried and upset about many things."

DEGREE OF OBSESSION

Jesus used a parable to talk about people who hold to material goods. It is our attitude toward "things," not what or how much we have, that determines our degree of obsession.

And He told them this parable: "The ground of a certain rich man produced a good crop. He thought to himself, 'What shall I do? I have no place to store my crops.'

"Then he said, 'This is what I'll do. I will tear down my barns and build bigger ones, and there I will store all my grain and my goods. And I'll say to myself, "You have plenty of good things laid up for many years. Take life easy; eat, drink and be merry." '

"But God said to him, 'You fool! This very night your life will be demanded from you. Then who will get what you have prepared for yourself?'

"This is how it will be with anyone who stores up things for himself but is not rich toward God" (*Luke 12:16-21*).

PRAYING TOGETHER

Choose the prayer that best fits your needs today and pray it during the group prayertime.

Lord, help me place less emphasis on material goods.

Father, thank You for the many things You have given me.

Father, help me worry less and trust You more.

Heavenly Father, help me be content with what I have.

THIS WEEK

This week, note "things" you purchase, "body" emphasis, and "people and animals" you give attention to.

THINGS	BODY	PEOPLE & ANIMALS

SEARCHING FOR ANSWERS 2

MEMORIES—WHAT DO I CHERISH?

SCRIPTURE

"Remember Lot's wife!" (*Luke 17:32*)

PURPOSE

To understand the role memories play in determining our behavior.

LOOKING INSIDE

1. Which emotion illustrated on page 6 best describes how you feel about childhood memories?

DISAPPOINTED

2. Which of your memories relate to certain times and places?

3. Which family heirlooms do you most treasure?

TIME AND PLACE

According to Dr. Russell W. Belk, "Most people . . . cherish childhood memories, both those remembered accurately and others." These are important but less tangible than material things ("My Possessions, Myself," *Psychology Today*, July/August, 1988, p. 52).

What are your most vivid childhood memories of occasions, places, cities, states, or countries?

Write out three important childhood memories.

#1

#2

#3

MEMORIES AND THINGS

The retail marketplace tries to take advantage of our memories, attempting to manipulate our buying habits. Television ads even use 30-year-old music to sell raisins!

Our memories are often attached to things. Identify five pieces of memorabilia about which you have changed your attitude over the years (for example: old family pictures, vases, dishes, or quilts).

1.

2.

3.

4.

5.

TAKE FIVE

With your neighbor, discuss an item you're glad you kept—one you now value because of attached memories.

PURSUITS

Read each Scripture passage and respond to the questions by underlining the answer.

What do the Scriptures tell us to pursue?

> For the love of money is a root of all kinds of evil. Some people, eager for money, have wandered from the faith and pierced themselves with many griefs. But you, man of God, flee from all this, and pursue righteousness, godliness, faith, love, endurance and gentleness (*1 Timothy 6:10-11*).

With whom should we place our hope?

> Command those who are rich in this present world not to be arrogant nor to put their hope in wealth, which is so uncertain, but to put their hope in God, who richly provides us with everything for our enjoyment (*1 Timothy 6:17*).

What are we told to do?

> Command them to do good, to be rich in good deeds, and to be generous and willing to share (*1 Timothy 6:18*).

Why are we told to do the above?

> In this way they will lay up treasure for themselves as a firm foundation for the coming age, so that they may take hold of the life that is truly life (*1 Timothy 6:19*).

What are we warned against?

> Then He [Jesus] said to them, "Watch out! Be on your guard against all kinds of greed; a man's life does not consist in the abundance of his possessions (*Luke 12:15*).

Who is blessed?

> The memory of the righteous will be a blessing, but the name of the wicked will rot (*Proverbs 10:7*).

How many of the things Scripture urges us to pursue deal with possessions and how many with relationships?

PRAYING TOGETHER

Choose the prayer that best fits your needs today and pray during the group prayertime.

Father, thank You for my childhood memories.

Dear Lord, help me in the pursuit of ______________________ (righteousness, godliness, faith, love, endurance, gentleness).

Heavenly Father, please be with me this week as I see others with things I don't have. Give me peace and contentment.

Father, help me gain a heavenly perspective on treasures.

Father, help me resist the temptations of advertisers who try to take advantage of my memories.

THIS WEEK

Select a belonging that holds memories for you, and bring it to the study next week.

3 SEARCHING FOR ANSWERS

MOTIVES—WHAT IS MY INTENT?

SCRIPTURE

"The worries of this life, the deceitfulness of wealth and the desires for other things come in and choke the word, making it unfruitful" (*Mark 4:19*).

PURPOSE

To clarify our perspectives on "things."

LOOKING INSIDE

1. Which emotion illustrated on page 6 best describes how you feel about something new your neighbor, close friend, or family member has purchased?

2. Which best illustrates your emotion as you contemplate the purchase of something you both want and need?

3. What one thing do you most regret purchasing . . . or not purchasing?

FINANCIAL PROBLEMS

Check all the following that you think contribute to financial problems.

____ 1. Wrong attitudes toward money.
____ 2. Living beyond one's means.

____ 3. Credit buying.
____ 4. Self-indulgence.
____ 5. The fallacy that accumulating material things leads to contentment and happiness.
____ 6. Lack of a budget.
____ 7. Wastefulness.
____ 8. Hurting others to gain money.
____ 9. Medical and hospital bills.
____10. Covetousness.
____11. Not working.
____12. Being resentful of not having more.

(The first six items of the list are taken from *The Billy Graham Christian Worker's Handbook,* World Wide Publications, 1984, p. 104.)

TAKE FIVE

Discuss with your neighbor one item from the list that is a financial problem for you.

TRUE WEALTH

When we hear the term "wealth," we immediately think of money, investments, possessions. But we all know that true wealth can be found in nonmaterial things—a new grandchild, graduation day, a great vacation. We know wealth goes far beyond material goods.

Circle what 1 Timothy 6:6 says will bring gain:

> But godliness with contentment is great gain.

In your own words, what does 1 Timothy 6:7 tell us about long-range gain and hoarding money?

> For we brought nothing into the world, and we can take nothing out of it.

Give some specific examples of the earthly and heavenly treasures mentioned in Matthew 6:19-20 and what might happen to them.

> Do not store up for yourselves treasures on earth, where moth and rust destroy, and where thieves break in and steal. But store up for yourselves treasures in heaven, where moth and rust do not destroy, and where thieves do not break in and steal.

TREASURE IN HEAVEN

Discuss the concept of treasures in heaven. Reading the following story will help.

ONE RICH POOR MAN

A tax auditor came, years ago, to a poor servant of the Lord to determine the amount of taxes he would have to pay.

"What property do you possess?" asked the auditor.

"I am very wealthy," replied the Christian.

"List your possessions, please," the auditor instructed.

"First, I have everlasting life (John 3:16). I also have a mansion in heaven (John 14:2). I have a peace that passes understanding (Philippians 4:7). I have a faithful wife (Proverbs 31:10). I have healthy, happy, obedient children (Exodus 20:12). I have true, loyal friends (Proverbs 18:24). I have songs in the night (Psalm 42:8). I have a crown of life (James 1:2). I have a Savior, Jesus Christ, who supplies all my needs (Philippians 4:19)."

The auditor closed his book and said, "Truly you are a very rich man, but your property is not subject to taxation."

(*A Man and His World*, Church Development Resources, Grand Rapids, Mich., 1988, p. 8)

PRAYING TOGETHER

For group prayertime, say a sentence prayer that meets your needs, or use one of these.

Father, help me be discerning as I make purchases.

Heavenly Father, show me how to put my finances in order.

Lord, help me plan a budget and stick to it.

Father, give me new eyes to see that things do not provide happiness.

Father, help me be conscious of things I am wasting.

THIS WEEK

Research is the first step in budgeting. Take that step by evaluating all your expenditures for the past four months. Total your checks and other receipts by category:

- ☐ household (rent or house payment, utilities, telephone, yard work)
- ☐ department stores
- ☐ automobile (car payments, gasoline, insurance)
- ☐ other credit
- ☐ insurance (health and life)
- ☐ food; entertainment
- ☐ miscellaneous

Next week be prepared to share one area of expenditures that surprised you and how you can change your spending in that area.

12:00

MORALS—WHY DO I WANT, WANT, WANT?

SCRIPTURE

"For the love of money is a root of all kinds of evil. Some people, eager for money, have wandered from the faith and pierced themselves with many griefs" (*1 Timothy 6:10*).

PURPOSE

To determine if the financial and moral choices we make are developing good character.

LOOKING INSIDE

1. Which emotion illustrated on page 6 best describes how you would feel about winning the lottery? How do you think you'd spend the money?

2. Which best illustrates your feeling (emotion) when you help someone else who is in financial difficulty?

3. What was your most difficult purchasing decision in choosing between two items?

HOW TO KNOW IF YOU WORSHIP MONEY

In what ways do the following statements apply to you?

1. You spend more time thinking about how to get money than on how to pursue excellence in your work.

2. You never seem to have enough.

3. You flaunt what you own.

4. You resent giving it to others.

5. You sin to obtain money.

(MacArthur, Jr., John. *The Danger of Loving Money,* Moody Press, Chicago, 1989, pp. 10–11.)

INVENTORY

Use the following to provide a perspective on your belongings.

1. List some of your possessions you use daily.

2. List five possessions you seldom if ever use.

3. What would you consider a valid ratio of possessions used to those not used? (For instance, 1:10 would mean one item that you regularly use for every ten that you seldom use.)

1:10

1:5

1:1

4. Where do you currently store things that you don't use?

5. How would you feel if you got rid of the things you don't use?

TAKE FIVE

With your neighbor, discuss which things you could give away and by doing so help others and begin to clean your home.

BIBLICAL GUIDANCE

Scripture provides guidance on how we should view the relative value of money. Read each and highlight or record the main points.

> But seek first His kingdom and His righteousness, and all these things [food, clothes] will be given to you as well (*Matthew 6:33*).

> The earth is the Lord's, and everything in it (*1 Corinthians 10:26*).

> Therefore, I urge you, brothers, in view of God's mercy, to offer your bodies as living sacrifices, holy and pleasing to God—this is your spiritual act of worship. Do not conform any longer to the pattern of this world, but be transformed by the renewing of your mind. Then you will be able to test and approve what God's will is—His good, pleasing and perfect will (*Romans 12:1-2*).

The following verses point out on whom we are to depend to meet our needs.

> I was young and now I am old, yet I have never seen the righteous forsaken or their children begging bread (*Psalm 37:25*).

> Trust in the LORD with all your heart and lean not on your own understanding; in all your ways acknowledge Him, and He will make your paths straight (*Proverbs 3:5-6*).

> And my God will meet all your needs according to His glorious riches in Christ Jesus (*Philippians 4:19*).

PRAYING TOGETHER

Sometimes the stress of our material wants and needs makes us feel abandoned by the God who is supposed to be providing so richly for us. Peter Marshall wrote this poem for those times when we feel forsaken ("Our Seeking God," *The Prayers of Peter Marshall*, Catherine Marshall, ed., Chosen Books, a division of Baker Book House Company, 1989).

> Our Father, sometimes Thou dost seem so far away, as if Thou art a God in hiding, as if Thou art determined to elude all who seek Thee.

Yet we know that Thou art far more willing to be found than we are to seek. Thou hast promised, "If with all your heart ye truly seek Me, ye shall ever surely find Me." And has Thou not assured us that Thou art with us always?

Help us now to be as aware to Thy nearness as we are of the material things of every day. Help us to recognize Thy peace with as much assurance as we recognize the sounds of the world around us.

We would find Thee now in the privacy of our hearts, in the quiet of this moment. We would know, our Father, that Thou art near us and beside us; that Thou dost love us and art interested in all that we do, art concerned about all our affairs.

May we become aware of Thy companionship, of Him who walks beside us.

At times when we feel forsaken, may we know the presence of the Holy Spirit who brings comfort to all human hearts when we are willing to surrender ourselves.

May we be convinced that even before we reach up to Thee, Thou art reaching down to us. These blessings, together with the unexpressed longing in our hearts, we ask in the strong name of Jesus Christ, our Lord. Amen.

THIS WEEK

Clean out at least one closet. Divide the contents into several piles: "give away," "throw away," and "keep." Choose a charity in town and donate your "give away" items. Be prepared to share your experience next week.

Searching for Answers 5

Masters—Whom Do I Serve?

SCRIPTURE

"No one can serve two masters. Either he will hate the one and love the other, or he will be devoted to the one and despise the other. You cannot serve both God and Money" (*Matthew 6:24*).

PURPOSE

To facilitate decisions about who or what is the central focus of our lives.

LOOKING INSIDE

1. Which emotion illustrated on page 6 best describes how you feel about loaning your car to a friend?

2. Which illustrates your feeling about something you can't have?

3. What is your most prized possession?

CHOICES

One choice we make daily is whether to hoard or share—our time, experience, money, goods, love. Are our choices the same as we would like others to make for us?

It reminds me of the teacher's counsel to an 8th-grader that God would want him to share.

"For example," he asked Timmy, "if you had two homes, would you share one with a homeless person?"

"Yes," was Timmy's reply.

"And if you had two cars, would you give one to a family without a car?"

"Sure."

"And if you had two baseball mitts, would you share one with a kid who didn't have one?"

"No," said Timmy, "I don't think I'd do that!"

"Well, if you'd share a house and a car, why not a baseball mitt?" the teacher asked.

"Because," said Timmy, "I *have* two baseball mitts."

Our choices must reflect what we'd like others to choose if we were the recipient.

Following are some choices we might face during any day. How would you choose? Circle T if the statement is true for you; F if it is false.

T	F	I'd never let a credit card balance exceed 30 days.
T	F	I believe in always buying a more expensive gift than I receive.
T	F	Being in debt never bothers me.
T	F	I spend too much on clothes.
T	F	My child's education is our most important expenditure.
T	F	I give a set amount to the church every month.
T	F	My husband is too materialistic.
T	F	I want my child to marry someone from a prominent family.
T	F	My spouse and I agree on major purchases.
T	F	I always buy a new car, never a used one.

Review your answers. Are you happy with the character that is described by them?

TAKE FIVE

With a neighbor, discuss one or two situations you would like to answer differently. Commit to making a conscious effort to reverse your thinking on those subjects, and report your progress next week.

HEARTITUDE

Men and women have had to face tough decisions literally as long as they've been on earth. Even Abraham, a truly God-fearing man, had to choose between God's will and a son (Isaac) whom he cherished. It's a well-known story, and we know God provided a way out, once He saw that Abraham's heart was right.

Read the following verses.

> I swear by Myself, declares the LORD, that because you have done this and have not withheld your son, your only son, I will surely bless you and make your descendants as numerous as the stars in the sky and as the sand on the seashore. Your descendants will take possession of the cities of their enemies, and through your offspring all nations on earth will be blessed, because you have obeyed Me (*Genesis 22:16-18*).

In your own words, summarize the result of Abraham's obedience to God.

Just as with Abraham and Moses, God often lessens our negative consequences—even provides positive rewards—when He knows we're willing to make the right choice. Have you had an experience in which God brought good out of a seemingly impossible situation?

GIVE IT UP

In the account of "the mission of Moses" found in Exodus, Moses asked several questions of God before he responded to God's call to lead the sons of Israel out of Egypt.

> Moses answered, "What if they do not believe me or listen to me and say, 'The LORD did not appear to you'?"
>
> Then the LORD said to him, "What is that in your hand?"
>
> "A staff," he replied.
>
> The LORD said, "Throw it on the ground."
>
> Moses threw it on the ground and it became a snake, and he ran from it. Then the LORD said to him, "Reach out your hand and take it by the tail." So Moses reached out and took hold of the snake and it turned back into a staff in his hand (*Exodus 4:1-4*).

Look closely at what God asked Moses to do. God asked Moses to throw down his staff. This was more difficult for Moses than it would be for us. To Moses, a shepherd, his staff stood for security, protection, rescue, and rest. He had to give all those things up at God's command. Then God told him to pick it up again, and when he did, he picked up God's staff, not his own. What a wonderful choice to make.

Ask yourself: Am I holding on to my staff or God's staff? What are some of the "staffs" you use for security instead of leaning on God?

If you are holding God's staff, it will bless Him, you, and others. Our choice is not between money and God, but which one comes first in our lives.

> Our first responsibility, then, is to examine our own hearts to see what money really means to us and to ask God to

reveal this essential truth. Does it mean security? Stability? Status? Freedom? Fulfillment of dreams? Or is it a way to express ourselves, to spend for fun, to give?

(Mayhall, Jack and Carole. "The Cash Clash," *Discipleship Journal,* Issue 53, vol. 9, no. 5, September/October, 1989, p. 35.)

PRAYING TOGETHER

For group prayertime, say a sentence prayer that meets your needs, or use one of these.

Heavenly Father, help me put money in proper perspective in my life.

Father, help guide my decisions this week. Be there when I am weak.

Father, help me to remove the things in my life I have placed too much emphasis on.

Lord, I give to You the things in my life just as Moses did and ask You to bless them and use them for Your greater glory.

Father, I release my will "to want" to You. Help me to be obedient to Your will for my life.

THIS WEEK

Paul tells us, "I know what it is to be in need, and I know what it is to have plenty. I have learned the secret of being content in any and every situation, whether well fed or hungry, whether living in plenty or in want. I can do everything through Him who gives me strength" (*Philippians 4:12-13*).

Paul learned to be content with God's strength.

This week when the material world slips into your heart, sit silently and pray to God for His help to overcome. Read the following poem.

WE'RE HUNGRY, LORD

We're hungry for something, Lord.
We have so much rich food and cake and candy for ourselves, but we're hungry.
People around us are so stiff and tight and hard to reach And they make us that way.
But we're hungry for something more.
People we know keep talking about great ideas, brilliant questions, and the problem of God's existence.
But we're hungry for You, not ideas or theories.
We want You to touch us, to reach inside us and turn us on.
There are so many people who will counsel us to death.
But we're hungry for someone who really knows You and has You, someone who can get so close to us that we can see You there.
We have so many things but we're hungry for You.
Deep, deep down inside we're hungry, even if we appear to be silly, lazy, or unconcerned at times.
We're hungry for Your kind of power and love and joy.
Feed us, Lord, feed us with Your rich food.

—Anonymous

(*Hymns for the Family of God,* Paragon Associates, Inc., Nashville, Tenn., 1976, p. 106.)

SEARCHING FOR ANSWERS 6

MAKING MY JOY COMPLETE—LEARNING TO GIVE

SCRIPTURE

"His divine power has given us everything we need for life and godliness through our knowledge of Him who called us by His own glory and goodness. Through these He has given us His very great and precious promises, so that through them you may participate in the divine nature and escape the corruption in the world caused by evil desires" (*2 Peter 1:3-4*).

PURPOSE

To clear up misconceptions about what the Scriptures say about giving, and to encourage a more fulfilling life through giving.

LOOKING INSIDE

1. Which emotion illustrated on page 6 best describes how you feel about someone who's been publicly praised for special acts of giving?

2. Which illustrates your feeling when you've given to a person or organization, but you haven't been recognized?

3. What is a really special nonmaterial gift you've received? Who gave it, and why was it so special?

PERSONAL RESOURCES

In five minutes, using the following chart, list all the tools in each category—talent, free time, expertise, things—that you have available to give to others. Leave the last two columns blank for now.

TALENT	FREE TIME	EXPERTISE	THINGS	HOW TO DELIVER	TO WHOM

Now take another few minutes to compare lists with a neighbor and get ideas for additional items on your list.

TAKE FIVE

Take five minutes to talk with your neighbor about ways to provide these resources, and some people or organizations you can offer your resources to. Record these ideas in the last two columns of the chart.

HANDLING GIVING

Instructions on church or charitable giving are often misunderstood and miscommunicated. The Bible is very specific about what to give, how much, to whom, and for what reasons. Answer the following questions, using the Scriptures as your guide.

1. Do you get credit based on the size of a gift?

> Jesus sat down opposite the place where the offerings were put and watched the crowd putting their money into the temple treasury. Many rich people threw in large amounts.

But a poor widow came and put in two very small copper coins, worth only a fraction of a penny.

Calling His disciples to Him, Jesus said, "I tell you the truth, this poor widow has put more into the treasury than all the others. They all gave out of their wealth; but she, out of her poverty, put in everything—all she had to live on" (*Mark 12:41-44*).

His master replied, "Well done, good and faithful servant! You have been faithful with a few things; I will put you in charge of many things. Come and share your master's happiness!" (*Matthew 25:23*)

2. Is giving easier if you have a lot?

"All these [commandments] I have kept," the young man said. "What do I still lack?"

Jesus answered, "If you want to be perfect, go, sell your possessions and give to the poor, and you will have treasure in heaven. Then come, follow Me."

When the young man heard this, he went away sad, because he had great wealth (*Matthew 19:20-22*).

Jesus looked at him and said, "How hard it is for the rich to enter the kingdom of God! Indeed, it is easier for a camel to go through the eye of a needle than for a rich man to enter the kingdom of God" (Luke 18:24-25).

3. May we give to impress others?

So when you give to the needy, do not announce it with trumpets, as the hypocrites do in the synagogues and on the streets, to be honored by men. I tell you the truth, they have received their reward in full. But when you give to the needy, do not let your left hand know what your right hand is doing (*Matthew 6:2-3*).

4. Is there a set amount to give?

Woe to you, teachers of the law and Pharisees, you hypocrites! You give a tenth of your spices—mint, dill and cummin. But you have neglected the more important matters of the law—justice, mercy and faithfulness. You should have practiced the latter, without neglecting the former (*Matthew 23:23*).

Remember this: Whoever sows sparingly will also reap sparingly, and whoever sows generously will also reap generously. Each man should give what he has decided in his heart to give, not reluctantly or under compulsion, for God loves a cheerful giver. And God is able to make all grace abound to you, so that in all things at all times, having all that you need, you will abound in every good work. . . . Now He who supplies seed to the sower and bread for food will also supply and increase your store of seed and will enlarge the harvest of your righteousness (*2 Corinthians 9:6-8, 10*).

5. Does it do us any good to hoard our money and possessions?

And He told them this parable: "The ground of a certain rich man produced a good crop. He thought to himself, 'What shall I do? I have no place to store my crops.'

"Then he said, 'This is what I'll do. I will tear down my barns and build bigger ones, and there I will store all my grain and my goods. And I'll say to myself, "You have plenty of good things laid up for many years. Take life easy; eat, drink and be merry."'

"But God said to him, 'You fool! This very night your life will be demanded from you. Then who will get what you have prepared for yourself?'

"This is how it will be with anyone who stores up things for himself but is not rich toward God" (*Luke 12:16-21*).

6. What do we gain from giving?

Give, and it will be given to you. A good measure, pressed down, shaken together and running over, will be poured into your lap. For with the measure you use, it will be measured to you (*Luke 6:38*).

Honor the LORD with your wealth, with the firstfruits of all your crops; then your barns will be filled to overflowing, and your vats will brim over with new wine (*Proverbs 3:9-10*).

7. Who benefits when we give?

The King will reply, "I tell you the truth, whatever you did for one of the least of these brothers of Mine, you did for Me" (*Matthew 25:40*).

He will reply, "I tell you the truth, whatever you did not do for one of the least of these, you did not do for Me" (*Matthew 25:45*).

Giving is much more than putting money in a church collection plate. It begins with our realization and admission that the money and "things" we possess belong to and come from God. It ends with each one of us unselfishly contributing our time and resources. Joy comes from giving, not from consuming.

PRAYING TOGETHER

For group prayertime, say a sentence prayer that meets your needs, or use one of these.

Lord, thank You for all Your blessings. Help me become a better steward.

I pray that I can become an eager giver.

I know I'm only using Your things, Father; I want to be generous with Your gifts to me.

I pray for opportunities to share my blessings with others.

I know __________ is struggling with her giving, Lord; give her a clear understanding of Your will for her.

IN CLOSING

On a 3 x 5 card, list at least three actions you will commit to that will help you change your buying habits, and three to change your giving habits.

You are the only one who will see the card. Put the card in an envelope, seal it, address it to yourself, and give it to your leader. The card will be mailed to you in six weeks, so you can gauge your success in changing.

LEADER'S NOTES 1
MYSELF—WHO AM I?

WELCOME

Welcome each woman to the group. Point out that this book includes Scripture, but they may wish to bring their own Bibles. Explain that you will be praying as a group using sentence prayers, with samples provided. Assure group members that participation in praying aloud is optional; whenever they feel comfortable, they may pray aloud.

PURPOSE

Have a volunteer read the opening Scripture and Purpose statement aloud.

LOOKING INSIDE

Question 1: Have participants tell which emotion(s) they chose. Then ask volunteers to share their feelings about how their self-concept is related to how their needs are being met daily.

Question 2: Discuss the illustrations that show how participants would like to feel. Encourage people to elaborate on their choices.

Question 3: As you discuss the benefits of thinking less about "things," invite group members to share why they joined this group and what they hope to get out of it.

ARE YOU A SHOPAHOLIC?

Give the group time to respond to the list of questions, checking all that are applicable. After reconvening, comment that, according to Walters, "Experts say that if you answer 'yes' to any five of the questions, your spending is out of control." Help is available through 175 chapters of Debtors Anonymous; for information write P.O. Box 20322, New York, NY 10025-9992, or call 212-642-8222.

Have volunteers read the paragraphs that follow. The characteristics mentioned are those contained in the previous list of questions.

OVERCOMING

Ask volunteers to read the list of ways to overcome compulsive shopping; stop to share people's personal experiences.

WHAT DEFINES YOUR IDENTITY?

In an article called "My Possessions, Myself" *(Psychology Today,* July/August 1988), Dr. Russell W. Belk, University of Utah graduate professor of business administration, tells us that our sense of self depends heavily on what we possess. We are in a very real way, extensions of the things we have, and that "we generally include four types of possessions in our personal sense of self: body and body parts, objects, places and time periods, persons and pets" (p. 51).

Allow time for participants to circle those things they feel help define their senses of self.

TAKE FIVE

Have each participant share with a neighbor which of the three categories ranks first, second, and third in her life.

PITFALLS

Take several minutes for participants to list by category the pitfalls of assessing one's self by possessions. Use the following if examples are needed.

THINGS	BODY	PEOPLE & ANIMALS
Envy Anxiousness Being less of a giver Greed	Foolish desires Self-abusive weight loss Self-indulgent Surgery Pride	Jealousy Possessiveness Living through children Neglecting own growth

MATERIALISM

Have a volunteer read Steve Thurman's definition of materialism. Discuss the definition, adding to it and sharing in what ways people agree or disagree with it.

DEGREE OF OBSESSION

Have a volunteer read Luke 12:16-21. Discuss the different attitudes toward possessions that are prevalent in our society.

Use the following statements to trigger discussion if needed.

- ☐ My possessions make me happy.
- ☐ Getting more will make me happy.
- ☐ Everyone else has things.
- ☐ I must keep up with the Joneses.
- ☐ My possessions describe who I am.
- ☐ I deserve what I have.

Ask volunteers to comment on which attitudes they feel most likely to adopt.

PRAYING TOGETHER

Take time for prayer. How much time you spend will depend on the size of your group. Praying may be new for some group members, so give them permission to not pray aloud until they feel comfortable. Have participants look at the printed prayers, select one, then individually read or say one aloud. As leader, be sure you pray only one sentence, modeling the behavior you expect of others.

THIS WEEK

Encourage group members to make notes on the chart provided, recording things they buy, emphasis they put on their bodies, and people and animals they pay attention to this week. Ask them to reflect on how their actions in these three categories influence or reflect their self-concepts.

LEADER'S NOTES 2
MEMORIES—WHAT DO I CHERISH?

BRIDGE

Bridge from Session 1 by asking volunteers to describe anything they listed on the chart regarding the emphasis they placed on "things," "body," or "people and animals" this past week. Make the point that not all we possess is undesirable. God promises us good things in abundance. Nonetheless, we must be careful not to worship possessions, but to keep our priorities right.

PURPOSE

Have a volunteer read the opening Scripture and Purpose statement aloud. Comment that we are told to "Remember Lot's wife" because she cherished worldly things and lost her life. (Briefly review the story from Genesis 19 if group members are not familiar with it.)

Lot's wife missed the message in two ways. She cared about the wrong things—her comfortable life and her possessions. And she didn't care about the right things—God's will and her family. The fact is, we all have comfort zones that can cause us to stagnate. Only by giving them up and moving on, as God directs us, will we truly gain the joy of abundant life.

Give an example from your experience, then ask group members if they have experiences they can share. To help them understand the role memories play in determining our behavior, refer to the Introduction or relate a personal experience.

LOOKING INSIDE

Have group members respond to the questions describing how their childhood memories relate to emotions, to times and places, and which family heirlooms they most treasure.

TIME AND PLACE

Have a volunteer read the opening paragraph, then allow time for participants to record three important childhood memories.

Allow participants time to share one of their memories. With each, point out whether the memory is tied to "things," "body," or "people and animals." In particular, stress those memories tied to time and relationships with people, which don't cost anything.

Don't rush through this time of sharing memories; this session is intentionally shorter than some to allow for the bond-building that comes from sharing personal stories with one another.

MEMORIES AND THINGS

Comment on how retail marketers exploit our memories. Then allow time for participants to list five things about which they have changed their attitudes over the years. Give personal examples, then take time for participants to share their lists. Comment that as we age we place higher value on heirlooms—things that provide a sense of the past and a link with prior generations.

Donna Otto, a time management consultant, suggests that as you consider throwing away, giving away, or keeping things, you not give away anything which could hold a memory.

TAKE FIVE

Allow five minutes for participants to discuss items they're glad they kept and now value because of attached memories.

PURSUITS

Have volunteers read the Scripture passages and respond to the questions by underlining the answers.

- ☐ What do the Scriptures tell us to pursue? (Righteousness, godliness, faith, love, endurance, and gentleness.)
- ☐ With whom should we place our hope? (Hope in God.)
- ☐ What are we told to do? (Do good, be rich in good deeds, be generous, be willing to share.)
- ☐ Why are we told to do the above? (To lay up treasure for a firm foundation, so that they may take hold of true life.)
- ☐ What are we warned against? (Greed, since a good life does not consist of an abundance of possessions.)

- ☐ Who is blessed? (The righteous.)

- ☐ How many of the things Scripture urges us to pursue deal with possessions and how many with relationships? (They all deal with relationships; the deeds could involve possessions, but only as they benefit someone else.)

PRAYING TOGETHER

Take about five minutes for prayer. This will vary depending on the size of your group. Since praying in a group may be new for many, use the printed prayers, allowing each person to select one. Close this special time together, modeling how to close a prayer: "In Jesus' name we pray. Amen."

THIS WEEK

Encourage each woman to bring some keepsake to the next group meeting.

LEADER'S NOTES 3
MOTIVES—WHAT IS MY INTENT?

BRIDGE

Bridge from Session 2 by having volunteers show and describe the item that holds a precious memory.

SCRIPTURE

Have a volunteer read the opening Scripture and Purpose statement aloud. Remind group members of the context of the verse by briefly reviewing the Parable of the Sower (Mark 4:1-10), then share a personal experience that validates the truth of the Scripture.

LOOKING INSIDE

Have group members volunteer responses to the three questions.

FINANCIAL PROBLEMS

Allow time for group members to check items on the list they think contribute to financial problems. Take time to discuss all twelve things that contribute to financial problems. Use the following Scriptures and your own experience to clarify or add to the discussion.

1. There's no way to "get rich quick." Recall the banking collapse in the '80s. See 1 Timothy 6:10.

2. Don't fool yourself about the ability to afford things. Prioritize needs and wants. Compare Luke 14:28-30.

3. Don't live on credit. See what it's done to America! Romans 13:8 and 2 Kings 4:7 give a biblical approach.

4. If you're self-indulgent, buying unnecessary things or feeding habits like smoking or drinking, be sure to understand and count the cost. See Luke 12:16-21 and Matthew 6:31-33.

5. Admit to yourself that material things have never produced long-lasting contentment. Refer to Luke 18:22-24.

6. Plan and budget. Price your priorities so you can stop spending when you've exhausted your income. See Proverbs 30:24-28, where the Scripture tells us the ants prepare by planning for the winter when they cannot get food.

7. "Waste not, want not" isn't just a saying; it's the truth. Individual wastefulness is a sin; our collective wastefulness is a national catastrophe. Compare John 6:12 and Matthew 18:7.

8. There can be no true peace in financial gain through hurting others. See Mark 12:40.

9. Medical costs are usually unplanned and can be catastrophic. Make sure you have the best insurance coverage you can afford, study your options, and seek advice before choosing treatment. One needs to prepare for the future by saving for medical and other emergencies, as Proverbs 21:20 points out.

10. Simply put, don't covet anything another person possesses. See Exodus 20:17.

11. Don't hide behind any excuse for not working. Honest work is scriptural. See Proverbs 28:19 and Proverbs 14:23.

12. Don't blame others or circumstances for your lack of material things. Pray for guidance, and give thanks for needs being met. See Philippians 4:11-13.

TAKE FIVE

Allow five minutes for participants to share with a neighbor one item from the list of twelve that is a financial problem.

TRUE WEALTH

Have different volunteers read the introductory paragraph and respond to the statements and notes.

TREASURES IN HEAVEN

Discuss the concept of treasures in heaven. Have volunteers read the story "One Rich Poor Man." Be prepared to read full Scriptures and respond to anyone who has a question regarding the possessions listed.

PRAYING TOGETHER

If your group is becoming comfortable praying aloud together, invite members to say sentences of their own making if they prefer that over using one of the printed prayers.

THIS WEEK

This can be a hefty and intimidating assignment for those who are out of touch with their finances. Some women in the group may defer all financial concerns to their husbands and not know where to begin. Assure them that this assignment is to help them get a better sense of where their money is going; they will not be expected to share personal financial details and the group will not evaluate them on their spending habits.

LEADER'S NOTES 4
MORALS—WHY DO I WANT, WANT, WANT?

BRIDGE
Ask for volunteers to share one area of expenditure that surprised them as they reviewed their spending for the last four months. Discuss what they might do to change their spending habits in that area.

PURPOSE
Have a volunteer read the opening Scripture and Purpose statement aloud.

LOOKING INSIDE
Allow members to "look inside" themselves and share their feelings on finances. If necessary, be the first to offer frank comments.

HOW TO KNOW IF YOU LOVE MONEY
Use the following notes from John MacArthur, Jr. (*The Danger of Loving Money,* Moody Press, Chicago, 1989, pp. 10–11) to guide your discussion.

1. "Are you more concerned with how much you make or the quality of your service? Is your job a means to finance your indulgences, or a means by which you can glorify God? Our response to daily tasks reveals much about whether we love money or not."

2. "A person who loves money is never satisfied with what he has. He hasn't learned to be content in whatever state he finds himself (Philippians 4:11)."

3. "People who love money derive an inordinate amount of pleasure from wearing, driving, living in, and showing off what they buy."

4. "It pains people to give even to a worthy cause when they're preoccupied with self-gratification. The idea of giving or sharing is distasteful to them."

5. "Some people will lie on their income tax returns, cheat on their expense accounts, steal from the till at their jobs, or compromise their convictions to obtain money. Any time you sin to get money, you prove that you love money more than you love God and His righteousness.

"If any of those statements reflect your actions and attitudes regarding money, be warned that such love for money will produce all kinds of evil in your life (1 Timothy 6:10). If you continue, you are succumbing to the deceitfulness of riches (Matthew 13:22)."

INVENTORY
Read each statement, pausing for participants to respond.

TAKE FIVE
Allow participants to discuss with their neighbor what "stuff" they could eliminate, and by doing so help others and begin to clean their own home. Mention something in your home as an example.

BIBLICAL GUIDANCE
Have volunteers read each Scripture passage. Draw out the following main points related to how we should view money.

Matthew 6:33—Seek God first.

1 Corinthians 10:26—Everything belongs to God.

Romans 12:1-2—Renew your mind instead of adopting the world's standards.

Psalm 37:25; Proverbs 3:5-6; Philippians 4:19—Depend on God, not material possessions.

PRAYING TOGETHER
Have group members read the prayer written by Peter Marshall. You may wish to close in a brief personal prayer for the group as well.

THIS WEEK
Review the assignment.

LEADER'S NOTES 5
MASTERS—WHOM DO I SERVE?

BRIDGE

Ask volunteers to tell about their closet-cleaning projects. What happened?

PURPOSE

Have a volunteer read the opening Scripture and Purpose statement.

LOOKING INSIDE

Encourage group members to share their feelings regarding their possessions—loaning possessions, those they can't have, and those that they most prize.

CHOICES

Have a volunteer read Timmy's story. Then read the choice statements, pausing after each to allow group members to make their choices.

TAKE FIVE

Have members discuss with their neighbor the choices that they wish they could make differently.

HEARTITUDE

Have volunteers read the paragraphs and following Scripture. Briefly review the story of Abraham's willingness to sacrifice Isaac (Genesis 22:1-18) if it is unfamiliar to some group members.

The purpose of this section is to show participants that we can trust God when we give in to His will. Ask if anyone can relate a personal experience in which good things resulted from an impossible situation, once they turned it over to God.

GIVE IT UP

We all hold on to what makes us feel happy, secure, and safe. Moses did also. Have volunteers read Exodus 4:1-4, then discuss the act of giving up.

Allow volunteers to describe the things that they turn to for security. Share a personal experience if appropriate.

Have a volunteer read aloud the quote from Jack and Carole Mayhall. Invite suggestions on how to carry out this personal assessment. Allow a few moments for individuals to reflect silently on the role money plays in their own lives.

PRAYING TOGETHER

Take about five minutes for prayer. The time will vary depending on the size of your group. Allow participants to use one of the printed prayers or give them a few moments to write their own.

THIS WEEK

Review the assignment.

LEADER'S NOTES 6
MAKING MY JOY COMPLETE—LEARNING TO GIVI

BRIDGE

Ask if anyone would like to share their reflections on the material world crowding their heart this past week. Allow time for people to report on their progress from last week's "Take Five" section.

PURPOSE

Have a volunteer read the opening Scripture and Purpose statement aloud.

LOOKING INSIDE

Have group members volunteer responses to the three questions.

PERSONAL RESOURCES

Allow five minutes for participants to fill in the first four columns of the chart, listing all the tools they have available to give. Fill in your chart and share it with the group.

Allow time for participants to compare lists with a neighbor and see if this spurs additional ideas for their lists.

TAKE FIVE

Allow five minutes for members to visit with their neighbors, this time filling in the "How to Deliver" and "To Whom" columns on the chart. Again fill in your chart and offer examples if needed.

HANDLING GIVING

Have everyone work through the questions individually, stopping after each to let a volunteer read and answer each question, then asking for additional comments from others.

Use the following notes to supplement or guide the discussion if needed.

1. The truth is, we should give because we love, and because Christ told us to give. We don't get any credit, except here on earth, if that's our objective.

2. a. Can you recall times when you gave thanks for good fortune?

   b. Do you give away personal or household items only when you no longer need or want them?

   c. Do you give so that, just like United Way, your class or small group can report 100 percent giving?

3. Not letting the "right hand" know what the "left hand" is doing does not mean we cannot record our contributions for legal tax deductions, although that should not be our motivation for giving. Nor does it mean that husbands and wives must keep financial secrets from each other.

4. Christ neither negates nor limits giving to the "law's" tithe. Motive and ability are the keys.

5. Good financial planning is not unscriptural. Fiscal maturity is an important facet of growth. However, we must caution against worshiping our riches.

6. This is as mysterious as any biblical teaching. Only when this life is over and we begin our eternal journey will we be able to reflect on and understand things that have happened to us.

7. We gain, but that should not be our motive. Joy and peace are **results** of pure motive, and are delivered by the Holy Spirit. True joy will not result from actions based on impure motives.

PRAYING TOGETHER

Take time for prayer using the printed prayers or allow time for participants to write their own.

IN CLOSING

Distribute 3 x 5 cards and envelopes, then instruct the group in the closing exercise.

RESOURCES

Books

Alcorn, Randy. *Your Money and Possessions.* Wheaton, IL: Tyndale House Publishers, 1989.

Blue, Ron. *Master Your Money.* Nashville, TN: Thomas Nelson Publishers, 1986.

Burkett, Larry. *The Complete Financial Guide for Young Couples.* Wheaton, IL: Victor Books, 1989.

_______. *Debt-Free Living.* Chicago, IL: Moody Press, 1989.

_______. *Investing for the Future.* Wheaton, IL: Victor Books, 1992.

_______. *What the Bible Says about Money.* Brentwood, TN: Wolgemuth and Hyatt Publishers, 1989.

Crosson, Russ. *Money and Your Marriage.* Dallas, TX: Word Publishing, 1989.

Bible Studies

Crown Ministries, 530 Crown Oak Center Drive, Longwood, FL 32750, (407) 331-6000. Training available to church members to lead a 12-week Bible study. Curriculum available from Crown.

Larsen, Dale and Sandy. *Moneywise.* Wheaton, IL: Harold Shaw Publishers, 1992.

MacArthur, John Jr. *The Danger of Loving Money.* Chicago, IL: Moody Press, 1989.

_______. *God's Plan for Giving.* Chicago, IL: Moody Press, 1985.

_______. *Overcoming Materialism.* Chicago, IL: Moody Press, 1983.

FIVE STEPS FOR ACCEPTING JESUS CHRIST AS YOUR PERSONAL LORD AND SAVIOR

"For God so loved the world, that He gave His one and only Son, that whoever believes in Him shall not perish but have eternal life" *(John 3:16)*

ACTION	SCRIPTURE	PRAYER	BENEFITS
1. ADMIT your need	Romans 3:23 Romans 6:23	Acknowledge you are a sinner	Eternal life
2. RECOGNIZE the provision	Romans 5:8 Romans 5:19	Acknowledge Christ died on the cross for you	Provides for your needs
3. ACCEPT forgiveness	Acts 3:19 Ephesians 2:8	Say you are sorry for your old ways and receive forgiveness	Eternal forgiveness
4. INVITE Christ into your life	Romans 10:13	Invite Christ into your heart	Continued relationship in prayer with a living God
5. COMMIT your life to Him	1 Peter 1:2 1 Peter 4:19 2 John 1:6 Psalm 37:4-5	Express your willingness to live for Christ, ask for His help to grow in your knowledge and understanding of Him and His will for your life	Obedience and a disciplined life with Christ will carry over to your personal and work life

DATE OF YOUR SPIRITUAL BIRTHDAY________________________

GOD'S GIFTS TO YOU	SCRIPTURE	PRAYER	BENEFITS
HOLY SPIRIT	John 14:14-18, 26 Hebrews 13:6 1 Corinthians 12:4 Matthew 7:11 Galatians 5:22	Thank God for the gift of the Spirit	Comforter Helper Giver of gifts Fruit of the Spirit
HIS PROMISES	2 Peter 1:3-4 2 Corinthians 12:9 Isaiah 40:31 James 1:5-8 1 John 1:7 Psalm 121:7-8 Isaiah 26:3-4	Ask Christ to reveal all things that are good and pure Give thanks for this special day	Security Power Strength Wisdom Fellowship Preservation Peace